OXFORD MEDICAL PUBLICATIONS

A Basic Formulary for General Practice

D1612996

PRACTICAL GUIDES FOR GENERAL PRACTICE

A Basic Formulary for General Practice

Practical Guides for General Practice 2

G. B. GRANT, D. A. GREGORY, and
T. D. van ZWANENBERG

*Department of Family and Community Medicine,
University of Newcastle upon Tyne*

Oxford New York Tokyo
OXFORD UNIVERSITY PRESS

Oxford University Press, Walton Street, Oxford OX2 6DP

Oxford New York Toronto
Delhi Bombay Calcutta Madras Karachi
Petaling Jaya Singapore Hong Kong Tokyo
Nairobi Dar es Salaam Cape Town
Melbourne Auckland

and associated companies in
Berlin Ibadan

Oxford is a trade mark of Oxford University Press

Published in the United States
by Oxford University Press, New York

First published 1987
Reprinted 1989

British Library Cataloguing in Publication Data

Grant, G. B.
A basic formulary for general practice.—
(Practical guides for general practice; 2)
—(Oxford medical publications)
1. Chemotherapy
I. Title   II. Gregory, D. A.   III. Van
Zwanenberg, T. D.   IV. Series
615.'8   RM262
ISBN 0–19–261616–1

Library of Congress Cataloging in Publication Data

Grant, G. B. (George Bryce)
A basic formulary for general practice.
(Practical guides for general practice; 2)
(Oxford medical publications)
Includes index
1. Chemotherapy—Handbooks, manuals, etc.
2. Family medicine—Handbooks, manual, etc. I. Gregory,
D. A. (David Andrew) II. Van Zwanenberg, T. D.
III. Title. IV. Series. [DNLM: 1. Drug therapy—
handbooks. 2. Formularies—Great Britain—handbooks.
QV 39 G7616]
RM262.G69   1987   615.5'8   86-31128
ISBN 0–19–261616–1 (pbk.)

Printed in Great Britain by The Alden Press, Oxford

Foreword

Prescribing is one of the most important professional activities that general practitioners undertake. The rational use of drugs requires doctors to prescribe effectively, safely, and economically. However, the task of making sensible choices from the large number of products which are made available by the pharmaceutical industry is daunting. Yet experience has shown that general practitioners require only a relatively small range of medicines to deliver the highest standards of clinical care to their patients.

In hospital practice the construction, adoption, and use of local formularies has become increasingly common. The most successful of these have developed as a result of discussion amongst the hospital staff. This formulary, specifically designed for the needs of general practice, is drawn on the experience of the general practitioners who teach medical students at the University of Newcastle upon Tyne. It is not just a recitation of recommended drugs; it provides information about when *not* to use drugs as well as offering sensible down-to-earth advice on both the selection and use of specific agents. It will be of value to established general practitioners, to trainees, and to medical students. Interestingly, and coincidentally, the authors have produced a list of products bearing close similarities to the WHO Essential Drugs List; I hope therefore that this formulary will reach an international audience. Written *for* general practitioners *by* general practitioners, it should occupy a special place in every doctor's black bag.

Michael Rawlins
Professor of Clinical Pharmacology,
University of Newcastle upon Tyne

Preface

This formulary was developed in order to provide simple and appropriate treatment for 90 per cent of the conditions presenting in general practice.

We compiled it in association with about twenty general practitioners who are Clinical Tutors to medical students at Newcastle University. These general practitioners came from different practices, and in a series of meetings (including a residential weekend) we modified and added to the formulary until a consensus was reached.

Advice of two consultant colleagues was obtained on specific matters.

The formulary is presented as an alphabetical list of conditions with the appropriate drug treatment, including dosage and price (cost, though important, was not regarded as the major consideration).

Except for a few proprietary combination preparations (e.g. oral contraceptives) we have used only generic names of drugs. In general, and only where there was strong evidence of a drug's superiority over other treatment, we have not included drugs which have been in use for less than five years.

We excluded most drugs which are used only in emergencies. Drugs normally initiated in a hospital are listed only in the appendix.

The list of conditions reflects the broad therapeutic areas seen in general practice, so that some conditions will be an actual diagnosis (e.g. asthma) and others will be symptoms (e.g. pain).

The more common skin conditions are also included.

We have specified what we think are the most appropriate drugs for each condition and have not normally included several drugs with identical actions. Where a choice of drugs *is* given, we have placed them in what we consider a sensible order. We have also set out some notes about diagnosis and the drugs. These notes are in no way meant to be comprehensive.

We know by controlled testing in several diverse practices that by using this formulary a general practitioner can prescribe for about 90 per cent of conditions encountered and which require a drug. This leaves the practitioner free to prescribe other drugs in special circumstances (e.g. drug-sensitivity, renal and hepatic disease).

We have also used this formulary in teaching medical students and they have found it of value.

It is easier and safer to become familiar with the action, side-effects, contraindications, and drug interactions of a limited number of well-proven preparations. We believe that a general practitioner using this formulary will be able to prescribe rationally, safely, and cheaply.

We hope you will find this pocket formulary of great use to you in your practice. We intend to revise the formulary at regular intervals, and would welcome suggestions and comments from readers.

Newcastle upon Tyne
1986

G. B. G.
D. A. G.
T. D. v. Z.

Acknowledgements

The authors would like to thank those many people who have assisted with the compilation of this formulary and without whose assistance it would not have been possible.

Over twenty general practitioners helped by recording their prescribing and by meeting on several occasions to reach a consensus on rational prescribing in general practice. This we believe makes the formulary a valid one and we would like to thank them all very sincerely.

We received sound advice and constructive criticisms from Professor J. H. Walker and Professor M. Rawlins which greatly encouraged us in our efforts, and Dr S. Comaish helped us with the dermatology section. Mr L. S. Ray, MPS, advised us on the pricing of drugs and gave a pharmacist's point of view.

Many others helped us but finally, without the skill, patience and long hours of work of Mrs Karen Cowley and Miss Anne Corradine the actual production of the formulary would never have been completed.

Proprietary drugs

Most of the drugs in the formulary are generic. However, some proprietary combination preparations are included:

All oral contraceptives
Alphosyl
Anusol
Betadine
Cyclo-progynova
Dithrocream
Dyazide
Gaviscon

Locorten-vioform
Maalox
Madopar
Nystaform HC
Polytar
Premarin
Pripsen
Sinemet

Contents

Abbreviations

amps	ampoules
BNF	*British National Formulary*
BP	*British Pharmacopoeia*
caps	capsules
CSM	Committee for the Safety of Medicines
CXR	chest X-ray
e.c.	enteric-coated
ECG	electrocardiograph
ESR	erythrocyte sedimentation rate
g	grams
Hb	haemoglobin
HRT	hormone replacement therapy
i.v.	intravenous
kg	kilogram
MAOI	monoamine oxidase inhibitors
mg	milligram
ml	millilitre
MSU	mid-stream urine specimen
s.r.	slow-release
suppos	suppositories
tabs	tablets
TSH	thyroid stimulating hormone
UTI	urinary tract infection
WBC	white blood count

Costing prescriptions

The cost of drugs (as at June 1986) is included, usually as the cost of 100 tablets/capsules or 500 ml for mixtures. This permits easy comparison. The actual cost to the National Health Service of any particular prescription can be calculated from the following formula.

	Formula	Example 28 capsules ampicillin 250 mg
(a) Cost of ingredients	x	84p
(b) On-cost of 9%	$9\%x$	8p
(c) Container	3p	3p
(d) Dispensing fee	55p	55p
(e) Approximate proportion of Basic Practice Allowance	10p	10p
	Total	£1.60p

It should be appreciated that the costs shown for prescriptions are only indicative and may vary slightly, depending on the volume of dispensing in a particular pharmacy.

It is proposed to change the basis of payment, and legislation has recently passed through parliament. The Basic Practice Allowance is to be discontinued (although an enhanced fee will be paid for the first 1350 scripts dispensed) and the on-cost will be reduced to a flat rate of 5 per cent. There should be little change in the cost of prescriptions.

The new contract militates against the smaller pharmacy and

may result in the number of pharmacies being reduced which could have an adverse effect on patient service.

The reduced on-cost will mean that pharmacists will have less of a financial interest in dispensing expensive products.

Allergy

Hayfever, Urticaria

Treatment

Chlorpheniramine	Adult dose:	4 mg three times daily.
	Child dose:	Under 1 year: 1 mg twice daily; 1–5 years: 1–2 mg three times daily; 6–12 years: 2–4 mg three times daily.
Terfenadine	Adult dose:	60 mg twice daily.
	Child dose:	30 mg twice daily (not recommended under 6 years of age).
Beclomethasone (nasal spray)	Adult and child dose:	50 micrograms to each nostril up to four times daily (not recommended under 6 years of age).

Prophylaxis

Sodium cromoglycate	Adult and child dose:	20 mg by nasal insufflation four times daily; or 2 per cent nasal spray four times daily (not recommended for children under 6 years); and/or 2 per cent eye drops four times daily.

Important notes

1. Chlorpheniramine, which is usually sedative, and terfenadine, which is rarely so, are alternative antihistamines. Either may be used in combination with beclomethasone spray and/or sodium cromoglycate.

2. Chlorpheniramine may potentiate the effects of alcohol and sedative CNS drugs. It may also cause other anticholinergic side-effects.

3. As sedation is possible, patients should be warned if driving or operating machinery.

4. Terfenadine has been in general use for less than 5 years. Any side-effects should be reported to the CSM.

5. Desensitizing injections are of doubtful benefit and may be dangerous.

Cost

Chlorpheniramine	4 mg	100 tabs	= £1.00
	2 mg/5 ml syrup	500 ml	= 97p
Terfenadine	60 mg	100 tabs	= £8.96
	30 mg/5 ml suspension	500 ml	= £10.00
Beclomethasone	Nasal spray	200 doses	= £4.77
Sodium cromoglycate	2% eye-drops	10 ml	= £4.19
	2% metered nasal spray	26 ml	= £5.36
	10 mg cartridge	100 caps	= £3.89

Anaemia

Treatment

Iron deficiency

Ferrous sulphate	Adult dose:	300 mg twice daily.
	Child dose:	Under 1 year: 60 mg three times daily;

| | | 1–5 years: 120 mg three times daily; 6–12 years: 200 mg three times daily. |
| Ferrous gluconate | Adult dose: | 300 mg twice daily. |

Vitamin B$_{12}$ deficiency

| | | |
| Hydroxocobalamin | Adult and child dose: | Initially: 1 mg repeated 5 times at intervals of 2–3 days; maintenance: 1 mg every 3 months. |

Folic acid deficiency

Folic acid	Adult dose:	Initially, 15 mg daily for 14 days; maintenance, 5 mg every 1–7 days.
	Child dose:	Up to 1 year: 250 micrograms/kg daily; 1–5 years: 2.5 mg daily; 6–12 years: 5 mg daily.

Important notes

1. Proper haematological diagnosis is essential.

2. Combined iron/folic acid preparations contain very little folic acid.

3. Large bowel malignancy is a common cause of iron-deficiency anaemia in the elderly.

4. Iron salts can cause gastrointestinal side-effects: nausea, epigastric pain, diarrhoea, or constipation.

5. Antacids and tetracyclines can cause reduced therapeutic response to iron preparations.

Cost

Ferrous sulphate	200 mg	100 tabs =	26p
	300 mg	100 tabs =	40p
	60 mg/5 ml mixture	500 ml	= £3.23

Ferrous gluconate	300 mg	100 tabs =	45p
Hydroxocobalamin	250 micrograms	5 amps =	46p
	1000 micrograms	5 amps =	90p
Folic acid	100 micrograms	100 tabs = £3.00	
	5 mg	100 tabs =	25p

Angina pectoris

Treatment

Nitrates

Glyceryl trinitrate	Adult dose:	500 micrograms as required.
or		
Isosorbide dinitrate	Adult dose:	10–40 mg three times daily.

Beta-blockers

Propranolol	Adult dose:	40–160 mg twice daily.
or		
Metoprolol	Adult dose:	50–200 mg daily in one or two doses.

Calcium antagonists

| **Nifedipine** | Adult dose: | 5–20 mg three times daily. |

Important notes

1. Treat predisposing causes: obesity, hypertension, anaemia, smoking, arrhythmias, etc.

2. Basic investigations: CXR; ECG; Hb; TSH; urinalysis.

3. Nitrates can cause flushing, headache, tachycardia, and syncope. Concurrent administration of phenobarbitone can reduce their effect. Should not be used 8 weeks after opening. No cotton wool in container.

4. Beta-blockers can cause bradycardia, heart failure, bronchospasm, peripheral vasoconstriction, gastrointestinal disturbances, vivid dreams, insomnia, and fatigue. They should not be used in asthma, heart failure, heart block, or intermittent claudication.

5. Withdraw nifedipine if angina worsens shortly after starting therapy.

6. Nifedipine side-effects are similar to those of glyceryl trinitrate but should be reported to CSM.

Cost

Glyceryl trinitrate	500 micrograms	100 tabs =	34p
Isosorbide dinitrate	10 mg	100 tabs =	£1.35
	20 mg	100 tabs =	£2.15
	30 mg	100 tabs =	£3.20
Propranolol	10 mg	100 tabs =	24p
	40 mg	100 tabs =	25p
	80 mg	100 tabs =	75p
	160 mg	100 tabs =	£1.15
Metoprolol	50 mg	100 tabs =	£4.71
	100 mg	100 tabs =	£8.75
Nifedipine	5 mg	100 caps =	£8.17
	10 mg	100 caps =	£12.19
	20 mg s.r.	100 caps =	£19.31

Anxiety/Agitation

Anxiety

Treatment

Diazepam	Adult dose:	2–10 mg twice or three times daily.
Propranolol	Adult dose:	10–40 mg twice or three times daily.

Important notes

1. Worry is not an illness, nor is unhappiness.
2. Look for depression.
3. Only short-term treatment with drugs is advised.
4. Benzodiazepine therapy of any kind can cause long-term dependence with subsequent withdrawal symptoms.
5. Benzodiazepines can cause nausea, constipation, drowsiness, dizziness, ataxia, confusion (especially in the elderly), depression, and occasionally rashes and blood dyscrasias.
6. For propranolol side-effects, *see under* beta-blockers, in Angina.
7. Lorazepam is addictive and should not be used as a first choice. Withdrawal should be with great care under diazepam cover.

Agitation

Treatment

Chlorpromazine	Adult dose:	10–100 mg three or four times daily.
	Child dose:	Up to 5 years: 5–10 mg three times daily; 6–12 years: $\frac{1}{2}-\frac{1}{3}$ adult dose.
Thioridazine	Adult dose:	25–100 mg three times daily.

Important notes

1. Extrapyramidal effects may occur with the major tranquillizers. These may by dose-related, related to the actual drug, or be due to patient idiosyncrasy.
2. Side-effects include dry mouth, constipation, hypotension (particularly in the elderly), inhibition of ejaculation, weight gain, hyperglycaemia, drowsiness, agitation, insomnia, depression, convulsions, Parkinsonism, tardive dyskinesia, urinary retention, rashes, and blood dyscrasias. Temperature regulation may be affected in the elderly.

Cost

Diazepam	2 mg	100 tabs =	12p
	5 mg	100 tabs =	13p
Propranolol	10 mg	100 tabs =	24p
	40 mg	100 tabs =	25p
Chlorpromazine	10 mg	100 tabs =	50p
	25 mg	100 tabs =	77p
	50 mg	100 tabs = £1.50	
	100 mg	100 tabs = £2.78	
	25 mg/5 ml syrup	500 ml = £2.20	
	10 mg/5 ml injection	10 amps = £2.95	
	25 mg/5 ml injection	10 amps = £1.84	
Thioridazine	10 mg	100 tabs = £1.13	
	25 mg	100 tabs = £1.86	
	50 mg	100 tabs = £3.60	
	100 mg	100 tabs = £6.95	

Arthropathies

Treatment

Aspirin e.c.	Adult dose:	300–600 mg four times daily.
	Child dose:	Not recommended for children under 12 years of age.
Ibuprofen	Adult dose:	200–600 mg four times daily.
	Child dose:	20 mg/kg weight daily, in divided doses.
Naproxen	Adult dose:	250–500 mg twice daily.
Piroxicam	Adult dose:	20 mg daily.

| Indomethacin | Adult dose: | 25–50 mg four times daily.
Rectally: 100 mg twice daily. |
| Triamcinolone | Injection | 2–30 mg according to site of lesion. |

Important notes

1. All non-steroidal anti-inflammatory drugs may cause nausea, vomiting, peptic ulceration, and haematemesis/melaena.

2. Aspirin may also cause tinnitus, deafness, urticaria, angioneurotic oedema, and bronchospasm.

3. Ibuprofen may also cause rashes and blood dyscrasias.

4. Piroxicam may cause similar side-effects to aspirin.

5. Indomethacin may also cause tinnitus, blurred vision, bronchospasm, depression, confusion, insomnia, peripheral neuropathy, convulsions, psychiatric disturbances, rashes, and blood dyscrasias.

6. Other drugs may be required, if the arthritis does not respond to the above drugs.

7. Triamcinolone local injection with or without lignocaine may be used in tennis elbow, etc.

Gout

Treatment

| Indomethacin
or | Adult dose: | 50 mg four times daily. |
| Naproxen | Adult dose: | 500–750 mg twice daily. |

Prophylaxis

| Allopurinol | Adult dose: | 100–900 mg daily. |

Important notes

1. Check serum uric acid before prophylactic treatment.

2. Concurrent indomethacin/naproxen advisable initially with allo-purinol.

3. Allopurinol may cause gastrointestinal irritation and rashes.

Cost

Aspirin e.c.	300 mg	100 tabs	= £2.10
	600 mg	100 tabs	= £3.53
Ibuprofen	200 mg	100 tabs	= £2.05
	400 mg	100 tabs	= £4.10
	600 mg	100 tabs	= £6.16
Naproxen	250 mg	100 tabs	= £10.85
	500 mg	100 tabs	= £20.78
	500 mg suppos	30 suppos	= £7.59
Piroxicam	10 mg	100 tabs	= £15.00
Indomethacin	25 mg	100 tabs	= £1.00
	50 mg	100 tabs	= £2.20
	100 mg suppos	30 suppos	= £7.29
Allopurinol	100 mg	100 tabs	= £4.74
	300 mg	100 tabs	= £18.39
Trimancinolone	20 mg/ml injection	1 amp	= £2.83
Lignocaine 1%	2 ml injection	1 amp	= 81p

Asthma

Treatment

Salbutamol	Adult dose:	*Oral:* 1–8 mg four times daily.
		Inhaled: 100–800 micrograms every 4–6 hours.

	Child dose:	*Oral:* 2–5 years: 1–2 mg four times daily; 6–12 years: 2 mg four times daily. *Inhaled:* 100 micrograms four times daily.
Theophylline s.r.	Adult dose: Child dose:	175–500 mg twice daily. 175 mg every 12 hours (over 6 years of age).
Prednisolone	Adult dose:	1–20 mg four times daily.
Beclomethasone	Adult dose:	*Inhaled:* 100–500 micrograms four times daily.
	Child dose:	50–100 micrograms four times daily.

Prophylaxis

Sodium cromoglycate	Adult and child dose:	2 mg four times daily (aerosol). 20 mg four times daily (insufflation).

Important notes

1. Advise the patient to stop smoking. Exclude possible extrinsic causative factors.

2. Salbutamol may cause palpitations, hypotension, tremor, and headaches. It should be used with caution in hyperthyroidism, ischaemic heart disease, hypertension, pregnancy, and elderly patients.

3. Measure serum theophylline concentration to check if within therapeutic range. Level may be variable and is critical. Caution: concomitant administration of i.v. aminophylline - particular care in elderly patients.

4. Theophylline may cause nausea, vomiting, vertigo, insomnia, confusion, and convulsions.

5. Corticosteroids including prednisolone have many serious side-effects with long-term use, the most important of which are: peptic ulceration, hypertension, fluid retention, diabetes, osteoporosis (especially in the elderly), mental disturbances, Cushing's syndrome, exacerbation of infections, and adrenal suppression.

6. Inhalation of beclomethasone may cause oral candidiasis and hoarseness.

7. Sodium cromoglycate may exacerbate acute asthma and should only be given prophylactically.

Cost

Salbutamol	2 mg	100 tabs =	92p
	4 mg	100 tabs =	£1.76
	8 mg	100 tabs =	£4.50
	2 mg/5 ml syrup	500 ml =	£1.96
	100 microgram inhaler	200 dose =	£2.18
	200 microgram cartridge	100 caps =	£5.29
	400 microgram cartridge	100 caps =	£7.15
Theophylline s.r.	175 mg	100 tabs =	£5.22
	250 mg	100 tabs =	£7.32
Beclomethasone	50 microgram inhaler	200 dose =	£4.77
	250 microgram inhaler	200 dose =	£7.32
	100 microgram cartridge	100 caps =	£7.26
	200 microgram cartridge	100 caps =	£9.67
Prednisolone	1 mg	100 tabs =	59p
	5 mg	100 tabs =	28p
Sodium cromoglycate	1 mg inhaler	200 dose =	£10.95
	20 mg cartridge	100 caps =	£10.07

Bronchitis

Treatment

Oxytetracycline	Adult dose:	250–500 mg four times daily.
Ampicillin	Adult dose:	250–500 mg four times daily.
	Child dose:	125–250 mg four times daily.
Co-trimoxazole	Adult dose:	960 mg twice daily.
	Child dose:	6 weeks to 6 months: 120 mg; 6 months to 5 years: 240 mg 6–12 years: 480 mg. All twice daily.
Erythromycin	Adult dose:	250–500 mg four times daily.
	Child dose:	125–250 mg four times daily.
Doxycycline	Adult dose:	200 mg on first day, then 100 mg daily.

Important notes

1. Tetracyclines should not be used in children under 12 years of age.

2. Tetracyclines and co-trimoxazole should not be used in pregnancy or lactation.

3. Oxytetracycline causes a rise in blood urea in renal impairment, but doxycycline does not. All tetracyclines including doxycycline can cause nausea, vomiting, and diarrhoea.

4. Ampicillin side-effects include urticaria, fever, joint pains, angio-neurotic oedema, anaphylactic shock in hypersensitive patients, and

diarrhoea. Ampicillin commonly produces a rash in patients with glandular fever and should not be prescribed if this is suspected.

5. Co-trimoxazole is a combination of 5 parts sulphamethoxazole and 1 part trimethoprim.

6. Co-trimoxazole may cause nausea, vomiting, rashes, Stevens–Johnson syndrome, agranulocytosis, purpura, and megaloblastic anaemia, particularly in the elderly.

7. Erythromycin may cause nausea, vomiting, abdominal pains, and diarrhoea in high doses.

8. The antibiotics included here are possible alternatives for the treatment of bronchitis, depending on the patient and likely causative bacteria.

Cost

Oxytetracycline	250 mg	100 tabs =	£1.08
Ampicillin	250 mg	100 caps =	£2.99
	500 mg	100 caps =	£5.92
	125 mg/5 ml suspension	500 ml =	£2.45
	250 mg/5 ml suspension	500 ml =	£4.60
Co-trimoxazole	480 mg	100 tabs =	£4.00
	240 mg/5 ml suspension	500 ml =	£8.00
Erythromycin	250 mg	100 tabs =	£4.50
	500 mg	100 tabs =	£20.67
	125 mg/5 ml suspension	500 ml =	£7.40
	250 mg/5 ml suspension	500 ml =	£11.15
	500 mg/5 ml suspension	500 ml =	£21.30
Doxycycline	100 mg	100 tabs =	£42.50

Cardiac failure

Treatment

Diuretics

Bendrofluazide	Adult dose:	2.5-10 mg in the morning.
Dyazide	Adult dose:	1-4 tabs in the morning.
Frusemide	Adult dose:	20-80 mg in the morning.
Spironolactone	Adult dose:	25-100 mg in the morning.

Cardiac glycoside

Digoxin	Adult dose:	62.5-500 micrograms daily.

Potassium replacement

Potassium chloride s.r.	Adult dose:	600-1200 mg three times daily.

Important notes

1. Dyazide is a combination of triamterene 50 mg and hydrochlorthiazide 25 mg.

2. With bendrofluazide and frusemide it may be necessary to give potassium chloride: the serum potassium should be checked at intervals.

3. Spironolactone can be given with frusemide to spare potassium loss.

4. Bendrofluazide may cause rashes, thrombocytopenia, and impotence.

5. Frusemide may cause rashes.

6. Spironolactone may cause gastrointestinal disturbances, and gynaecomastia and should be used with caution in pregnancy.

7. Digoxin toxicity is more likely in the elderly, in those with poor renal function and in hypokalaemia. Check serum digoxin especially if concomitant diuretic therapy.

8. Digoxin may cause anorexia, nausea, vomiting, visual disturbances, arrhythmias, heart block, malaise, and depression.

Cost

Bendrofluazide	2.5 mg	100 tabs =	40p
	5 mg	100 tabs =	21p
Frusemide	20 mg	100 tabs =	£3.24
	40 mg	100 tabs =	50p
Spironolactone	25 mg	100 tabs =	£5.95
	50 mg	100 tabs =	£14.20
	100 mg	100 tabs =	£24.60
Dyazide		100 tabs =	£6.32
Digoxin	all strengths	100 tabs =	86p
Potassium chloride s.r.	600 mg	100 tabs =	50p

Constipation

Treatment

Bulk laxative

Ispaghula husk	Adult dose:	2 teaspoonfuls in water once or twice daily.
	Child dose:	$\frac{1}{2}$-1 teaspoonful in water once or twice daily.

Stimulant laxative

Senna tablets	Adult dose:	7.5–30 mg at night.
	Child dose:	Half adult dose.

Faecal softener
Docusate sodium   Adult dose: 50–500 mg daily, in
                                        divided doses.
                        Child dose: 12.5–25 mg three times
                                        daily.

Osmotic laxative
Lactulose   Adult dose: 15 ml twice daily.
                        Child dose: Under 1 year: 2.5 ml
                                        twice daily;
                                        1–5 years: 5 ml twice
                                        daily;
                                        6–12 years: 10 ml twice
                                        daily.

Suppositories
Glycerol   Adult dose: 1 large or medium
                                        suppository daily.
                        Child dose: 1 small suppository
                                        daily.

Important notes

1. Dietary change to high fibre. Regular bran may be the long-term solution.

2. Anal fissure can cause acute constipation in children.

3. Chronic constipation in children often warrants specialist referral.

4. Regular bowel habits are important.

5. All laxatives are contraindicated if intestinal obstruction is suspected.

6. Ispaghula husk is contraindicated in faecal impaction and colonic atony: it may cause flatulence and intestinal obstruction.

7. Stimulant laxatives should not be prescribed for prolonged use. They should be avoided in children and pregnancy.

8. Docusate may colour urine red, and may cause excoriation and irritation if in prolonged contact with the skin.

Cost

Ispaghula husk	200 g	200 g =	97p
Senna tablets *B.P.*	7.5 mg	100 tabs =	90p
Docusate sodium	100 mg	100 tabs = £2.76	
	50 mg/5 ml syrup	500 ml = £3.75	
Lactulose	syrup	500 ml = £3.23	
Glycerol	small	5 suppos =	41p
suppositories	medium	5 suppos =	45p
	large	5 suppos =	95p

Contraception

The Pill

Treatment

Combined

Brevinor/Ovysmen	Dose:	1 daily for 21 days in every 28.
Microgynon 30/ Ovranette	Dose:	1 daily for 21 days in every 28.

Phased

Logynon/Trinordiol	Dose:	1 daily for 21 days in every 28.

Progesterone only

Micronor	Dose:	1 daily continuously.
Neogest	Dose:	1 daily continuously.

Morning-after Pill

Eugynon 50/Ovran	Dose:	Two tablets within 72 hours of intercourse, repeated after 12 hours.

Important notes

1. Check blood pressure twice yearly, cervical smear five-yearly.

2. The risk of thrombo-embolic and cardiovascular complications with the combined pill increases with oestrogen content, age, duration of therapy, obesity, smoking, and pre-existing medical conditions.

3. Side-effects of the combined pill are nausea, vomiting, headache, breast tenderness, changes in body weight, thrombosis, changes in libido, depression, chloasma, hypertension, impairment of liver function, benign hepatic tumours, reduced menstrual loss, spotting, and amenorrhoea.

4. Concomitant treatment with broad spectrum antibiotics, carbamazepine, chlordiazepoxide, neomycin, phenobarbitone, phenytoin, primidone, and rifampicin may produce contraceptive failure.

5. Combined preparations are contraindicated in pregnancy, history of thrombo-embolic disease, liver disease, severe migraine, undiagnosed vaginal bleeding, and mammary or endometrial carcinoma.

6. Progesterone-only preparations are to be used with caution in diabetes, hypertension, cardiac disease, functional ovarian cysts, malabsorption syndromes, and severe migraine. They should not be used in pregnancy, liver disease, carcinoma of breast, or other sex-hormone-dependent cancers.

7. Other contraindications include herpes gestationis and deteriorating otosclerosis.

Cost

Brevinor	1 pack = 52p
Eugynon 50	1 pack = 72p
Logynon	1 pack = 80p
Microgynon 30	1 pack = 49p
Micronor	1 pack = 63p
Neogest	1 pack = 78p
Ovran	1 pack = 29p
Ovranette	1 pack = 52p
Ovysmen	1 pack = 53p
Trinordiol	1 pack = 91p

Depression

Treatment

Tricyclic drugs

Amitryptiline	Adult dose:	50-100 mg at night.
Dothiepin	Adult dose:	75-150 mg at night.
Imipramine	Adult dose:	25-50 mg three times daily.
Protryptiline	Adult dose:	5-10 mg three times daily.
Clomipramine	Adult dose:	10-150 mg three times daily.

Tetracyclic drug

Mianserin	Adult dose:	10-30 mg three times daily, or as a single dose at night.

Important notes

1. Unhappiness is not a disease.

2. Amitryptiline and dothiepin are sedative. Imipramine is less so. Protryptiline stimulates.

3. Clomipramine is used for obsessive/compulsive neurosis associated with depression.

4. Tricyclics can cause dry mouth, metallic taste, constipation, nausea, vomiting, weight loss, tachycardia, arrhythmias, hypertension, impotence, blurred vision, glaucoma, drowsiness, tremor, fits, extra-pyramidal effects, delirium, hypomania, urinary retention, rashes, and blood dyscrasias.

5. Tricyclics interact with a number of drugs including anticholinergics, levodopa, methyldopa, MAOI.

6. Mianserin has fewer drug interactions; is much less cardiotoxic than the tricyclics but may cause skin rashes, arthralgia, convulsions, headache and leucopenia. Check WBC after 6 weeks use. It is safer in overdose.

Cost

Amitryptiline	10 mg	100 tabs =	64p
	25 mg	100 tabs =	88p
	50 mg	100 tabs =	£2.95
Dothiepin	25 mg	100 tabs =	£4.68
	75 mg	100 tabs =	£12.67
Imipramine	10 mg	100 tabs =	£1.65
	25 mg	100 tabs =	£3.15
Protryptiline	5 mg	100 tabs =	£1.83
	10 mg	100 tabs =	£2.71
Clomipramine	10 mg	100 tabs =	£3.46
	25 mg	100 tabs =	£6.81
	50 mg	100 tabs =	£12.95
Mianserin	10 mg	100 tabs =	£6.47
	20 mg	100 tabs =	£12.94
	30 mg	100 tabs =	£19.41

Diarrhoea

Treatment

Sodium chloride **and** glucose oral powder*	Adult and child dose:	1 powder to 200 ml water, taken liberally.
Codeine phosphate	Adult dose:	15-60 mg every 4 to 6 hours.
Sulphasalazine	Adult dose:	500 mg to 1 g four times daily.
	Child dose:	20-30 mg/kg daily in divided doses.
Erythromycin	Adult dose:	250-500 mg four times daily.
	Child dose:	125-250 mg four times daily.

Important notes

1. The basic treatment for acute diarrhoea is rehydration. No solid food or milk for at least 24 hours.

*2. Although listed in the *British National Formulary*, the generic form of sodium chloride and glucose powders is rarely available. The chemists may dispense more expensive proprietary preparations.

3. Sulphasalazine is only used in proven cases of ulcerative colitis and colonic Crohn's disease. It is a sulphonamide - beware possible allergy.

4. Erythromycin is only used in proven cases of campylobacter enteritis. As a rule antibiotics should not be used in cases of diarrhoea. For erythromycin side-effects, *see under* Bronchitis.

Cost

Sodium chloride **and** glucose oral powder	Proprietaries only are priced	24 powders = £4.00

Codeine phosphate	15 mg	100 tabs = £1.51
	30 mg	100 tabs = £1.51
	60 mg	100 tabs = £1.53
Sulphasalazine	500 mg	100 tabs = £7.01
Erythromycin	250 mg	100 tabs = £4.50
	125/5 ml syrup	500 ml = £4.68

Dyspepsia

Treatment

Magnesium trisilicate	Adult dose:	5-10 ml four times daily.
	Child dose:	5 ml four times daily.
Maalox	Adult dose:	10-20 ml after meals and at bedtime.
	Child dose:	Not used in children.
Aluminium hydroxide	Adult dose:	5-10 ml four times daily.
	Child dose:	Not used in children.

Duodenal/Gastric ulcer

Treatment

Antacids	As above	
Cimetidine	Adult dose:	400 mg twice daily for 4-6 weeks, then 400 mg at night.
	Child dose:	20-40 mg/kg twice daily.

Hiatus hernia/Reflux oesophagitis

Treatment

Gaviscon	Adult dose:	10-20 ml four times daily.

	Infant dose:	$\frac{1}{2}$-1 sachet mixed with feeds.
Metoclopramide	Adult dose:	10 mg three times daily.
	Child dose:	Should not be used in children.

Important notes

1. Small frequent meals: no smoking: reduce alcohol: improve posture.

2. 4 per cent gastric ulcers are malignant. Consider endoscopy, as malignant ulcers may cease producing symptoms initially with cimetidine.

3. Aluminium compounds constipate while magnesium compounds are laxative. Maalox is a combination of both.

4. Antacids may interfere with other drugs taken concurrently.

5. Cimetidine should be used with caution in renal disease, pregnancy, and with anticoagulants and phenytoin.

6. Cimetidine may cause gynaecomastia, loss of libido, and (less commonly) rashes, blood dyscrasias, and CNS symptoms.

7. Cimetidine, being an enzyme inhibitor, may cause reactions when used with other drugs, e.g. diazepam, warfarin, and metoprolol.

8. Metoclopramide caution: extrapyramidal effects occur particularly in the young, especially females. It enhances the effect of levodopa.

Cost

Magnesium trisilicate	mixture	500 ml	=	49p
Maalox	suspension	500 ml	=	£2.76
Aluminium hydroxide	mixture	500 ml	=	51p
Gaviscon	liquid	500 ml	=	£2.88
	sachets	10 sachets	=	£1.64
Cimetidine	200 mg	100 tabs	=	£14.83
	400 mg	100 tabs	=	£29.66
Metoclopramide	10 mg	100 tabs	=	£8.83

Endocrine conditions

Diabetes mellitus (non-insulin-dependent)

Treatment

Glibenclamide	Adult dose:	2.5–15 mg daily in the morning.
or		
Tolbutamide	Adult dose:	0.5–1.5 g in divided doses.
Metformin	Adult dose:	500–1000 mg three times daily.

Important notes

1. Diet alone is first line of treatment.

2. Glibenclamide and tolbutamide may encourage weight gain, should not be used in breast-feeding, and should be used with caution in the elderly or in renal failure because of the danger of hypogly-caemia. In the latter two cases tolbutamide is preferred. Sensitivity reactions may occur.

3. Use metformin in obese patients. Caution: lactic acidosis.

Cost

Glibenclamide	2.5 mg	100 tabs = £5.50
	5 mg	100 tabs = £9.20
Tolbutamide	500 mg	100 tabs = £1.31
Metformin	500 mg	100 tabs = £2.51
	850 mg	100 tabs = £4.00

Hypothyroidism

Treatment

Thyroxine   Adult and child dose: 50–200 micrograms
                                                 daily.

Important notes

1. Caution cardiac conditions.
2. Monitor TSH levels to achieve correct dose, and then annually.

Cost

Thyroxine   25 micrograms   100 tabs = 20p
                         50 micrograms   100 tabs = 27p
                         100 micrograms   100 tabs = 34p

Eye conditions

Blepharitis/Conjunctivitis

Treatment

Chloramphenicol   Adults and children: Apply every 3–6 hours.
  eye-drops or
  ointment

Sulphacetamide   Adults and children: Apply every 3–6 hours.
  eye-drops or
  ointment

Dry eyes

Treatment

Hypromellose eye-drops	Adults and children:	2 drops every 6 hours.

Dendritic corneal ulcer

Treatment

Idoxuridine eye-drops	Adults and children:	2 drops every 1–4 hours.

Important notes

1. Caution: *Painful red eye* – consider referral.

2. Seek history of foreign body or trauma. Use 1 per cent fluorescein drops to detect corneal abrasion or ulcer.

3. Do not use corticosteroid drops.

4. Allergic conditions or dry eyes can cause irritation.

5. Eye-drops are subject to bacterial contamination. Discard them after four weeks.

Cost

Chloramphenicol	eye-drops		10 ml =	£1.05
	ointment		4 g =	61p
Sulphacetamide	eye-drops	10%	10 ml =	80p
		20%	10 ml =	82p
		30%	10 ml =	83p
	ointment	2.5%	4 g =	54p
		6%	4 g =	57p
		10%	4 g =	59p
Hypromellose	eye-drops		10 ml =	£1.04
Idoxuridine	eye-drops		15 ml =	£3.35

Hypertension

Treatment

Diuretic
Bendrofluazide   Adult dose: 2.5–5 mg every morning.

Beta-blockers
Atenolol   Adult dose: 50–100 mg daily.
  or
Metroprolol   Adult dose: 50–100 mg twice daily.
  or
Propranolol   Adult dose: 10–160 mg twice daily.

Vasodilator
Hydralazine   Adult dose: 25–100 mg twice daily.

Calcium antagonist
Nifedipine s.r.   Adult dose: 20–40 mg twice daily.

Alpha-blocker
Prazosin   Adult dose: 500 micrograms to 20 mg daily, in divided doses.

Centrally-acting
Methyldopa   Adult dose: 250 mg to 1 g four times daily.

Important notes

1. Basic investigations: CXR, ECG, urea, creatinine, MSU, urinalysis.

2. Underlying conditions such as renal disease, coarctation, Conn's syndrome, etc., warrant referral.

3. Drugs acting in different ways may be used either singly or in combination.

4. Bendrofluazide may cause hypokalaemia, and potassium supplements may be necessary. It may also cause hyperuricaemia, hyperglycaemia, impotence, and skin rash.

5. Beta-blockers, particularly propranolol, may cause bronchospasm and should be used with caution in patients with asthma. They may also cause fatigue, bradycardia, vivid dreams, congestive heart failure, Raynaud's phenomenon, impotence, and worsening claudication.

6. Hydralazine should only be given with a beta-blocker and/or bendrofluazide, and should not be given to slow acetylators. These patients may be identified by testing heparinized blood taken 24 hours after 100 mg of Dapsone. Check with your local clinical pharmacologists. Hydralazine may cause facial flushing, weight gain, headache, tachycardia, possibly angina, and drug-induced lupus syndrome.

7. Nifedipine may cause throbbing headache, flushing, postural hypotension, and tachycardia.

8. The first dose of prazosin should be small, as it may cause profound hypotension and syncope. Increasing doses should also be small.

9. Methyldopa may cause dry mouth, sedation, depression, drowsiness, diarrhoea, impotence, liver damage, and lupus syndrome. It is contraindicated in patients with depression, active liver disease, and phaeochromocytoma.

10. Many doctors might commence treatment with bendrofluazide or a beta-blocker and then use them in combination if the blood pressure is not satisfactorily controlled. To this combination nifedipine or hydralazine may be added if necessary. Prazosin or methyldopa may be used for patients in whom the other drugs are contraindicated or ineffective.

Cost

Bendrofluazide	2.5 mg	100 tabs =	40p
	5 mg	100 tabs =	59p
Atenolol	50 mg	100 tabs =	£17.43
	100 mg	100 tabs =	£24.93
Metroprolol	50 mg	100 tabs =	£4.71
	100 mg	100 tabs =	£8.75

Propranolol	10 mg	100 tabs =	24p
	40 mg	100 tabs =	25p
	80 mg	100 tabs =	75p
	160 mg	100 tabs =	£1.15
Hydralazine	25 mg	100 tabs =	£1.56
	50 mg	100 tabs =	£3.06
Nifedipine s.r.	20 mg	100 tabs =	£19.31
Prazosin	500 micrograms	100 tabs =	£4.08
	1 mg	100 tabs =	£5.25
	2 mg	100 tabs =	£6.98
Methyldopa	125 mg	100 tabs =	£3.87
	250 mg	100 tabs =	£2.46
	500 mg	100 tabs =	£5.44

Insomnia

Treatment

Temazepam	Adult dose:	10–40 mg at night.
	Elderly patients:	5–15 mg at night.
Nitrazepam	Adult dose:	5–10 mg at night.
	Elderly patients:	2.5–5 mg at night.
Chlormethiazole	Adult dose:	192–500 mg at night.
Promethazine	Adult dose:	25–75 mg at night.
	Child dose:	6–12 months: 10 mg at night;
		1–5 years: 15–20 mg at night;
		6–10 years: 20–25 mg at night.
Trimeprazine	Child dose:	3 mg/kg at night.

Important notes

1. The cause of insomnia should be established and underlying factors such as pain, anxiety, or depression should be treated.

2. Hypnotics can cause confusion (especially in the elderly), dependence, hangover, and rebound sleeplessness on withdrawal. They should only be prescribed in short courses for patients with acute distress.

3. Temazepam has a shorter half-life than nitrazepam and therefore causes less hangover. Both can cause drowsiness, dizziness, ataxia, and confusion.

4. Chlormethiazole is less cumulative than nitrazepam and may be safer in pregnancy and in nursing mothers or elderly patients.

5. Promethazine and trimeprazine are antihistamines and are the only hypnotics suitable for children. Short-term use only is advisable, except in cases of severe pruritus or allergy. Side-effects include drowsiness, irritability, headache, vomiting, and anticholinergic effects such as dry mouth and blurred vision. Paradoxical stimulation may rarely occur.

Cost

Temazepam	10 mg	100 caps	= £4.80
	20 mg	100 caps	= £7.60
	10 mg/5 ml elixir	500 ml	= £6.00
Nitrazepam	5 mg	100 tabs	= 98p
	10 mg	100 tabs	= £1.88
	2.5 mg/5 ml mixture	500 ml	= £6.40
Chlormethiazole	192 mg	100 caps	= £4.62
	250 mg/5 ml syrup	500 ml	= £5.93
Promethazine	10 mg	100 tabs	= £1.72
	25 mg	100 tabs	= £2.38
	5 mg/5 ml elixir	500 ml	= £3.35
Trimeprazine	10 mg	100 tabs	= £2.58
	7.5 mg/5 ml syrup	500 ml	= £3.41
	30 mg/5 ml syrup	500 ml	= £7.28

Irritable bowel syndrome

Treatment

Mebeverine   Adult dose: 135 mg three times
                                          daily before meals.

Important notes

1. Any psychological problems should be discussed with the patient.
2. A high-fibre diet with plentiful fluid intake is advisable.
3. The need for rectal examination, full blood count, liver function tests, barium studies, and endoscopy should be considered before making the diagnosis.
4. Mebeverine is well tolerated and is without serious side-effect.

Cost

Mebeverine   135 mg   100 tabs = £8.35

Anal discomfort

Treatment

Anusol   Adult dose: 1 suppository or
                                          application of cream
                                          or ointment twice
                                          daily and after
                                          defaecation.

Important notes

1. Anal discomfort is a common symptom of patients suffering from haemorrhoids, fissure-in-ano, and proctitis. Patients should be advised to avoid constipation and pay careful attention to local hygiene.
2. Anusol is a mixture of bismuth oxide, bismuth subgallate, zinc oxide, and Peru balsam.

Cost

Anusol	cream	23 g = 86p
	ointment	25 g = 82p
	2.8 g suppos	12 = 88p

Menopause

Treatment

Premarin	625 micrograms to 2.5 mg daily from 5th to 25th day of cycle.
or	
Cyclo-progynova	One tablet daily from 5th to 26th day of cycle.
Clonidine	50 micrograms twice daily.
Dienoestrol cream 0.01%	Insert 1-2 applicatorfuls daily for 1-2 weeks, and then 1 applicatorful one to three times weekly as required.

Important notes

1. Most menopausal women do not require hormone replacement therapy or other treatment. Flushing and pruritus vulvae are the two symptoms most amenable to treatment.

2. Premarin consists of conjugated oestrogens whereas Cyclo-progynova contains oestrogen and progestogen (11 tablets of oestradiol 1 mg and 10 tablets of combined oestradiol 1 mg and levonorgestrel 250 micrograms).

3. Oestrogen therapy is associated with an increased risk of thromboembolic disease and endometrial carcinoma.

4. There is no withdrawal bleeding if oestrogens are used alone. The addition of a progestogen may modify the potentially harmful effect of oestrogen on the endometrium. However, the combined preparation produces withdrawal bleeding, which many menopausal women find a major nuisance.

5. Prescribing hormone replacement therapy for menopausal women demands the same care as the prescription of the combined contraceptive for younger women, as the side-effects and contraindications are the same (*see* Contraception).

6. Patients who have been on any form of oestrogen replacement therapy for two years should be referred for diagnostic endometrial curettage.

7. Clonidine may be useful to alleviate flushing in patients unable to take hormone replacement therapy. It can cause dry mouth and sleeplessness and may aggravate depression.

8. Dienoestrol cream is useful local treatment for vaginal dryness or discomfort.

Cost

Premarin	625 micrograms	100 tabs = £4.48
	1.25 mg	100 tabs = £7.31
	2.5 mg	100 tabs = £9.51
Cyclo-progynova	1 mg	21 tabs = £2.83
Clonidine	25 micrograms	100 tabs = £5.11
Dienoestrol	0.01% cream	78 g = £2.44

Migraine

Treatment

Soluble aspirin	Adult dose:	600 mg immediately and six-hourly as required.
or	Child dose:	Not recommended for children under 12.
Soluble paracetamol	Adult dose:	1 g immediately and six-hourly as required.

	Child dose:	6–12 years: 250–500 mg immediately, and six-hourly as required.
Metoclopramide	Adult dose:	Under 20 years: 5 mg three times daily. Over 20 years: 10 mg three times daily.
	Child dose:	Not recommended for children under 15.

Prophylaxis

Clonidine	Adult dose:	50 micrograms twice daily.
Propranolol	Adult dose:	40 mg twice daily.
Pizotifen	Adult dose:	1.5 mg at night or 500 micrograms three times daily.
	Child dose:	Up to 1.5 mg daily; maximum single dose at night 1 mg.

Important notes

1. Elucidate and avoid any precipitating factors. Combined oral contraceptives may cause or worsen migraine.

2. Gastric motility is reduced once the migraine becomes established. Patients should be advised to take aspirin or paracetamol with metoclopramide, which promotes gastric emptying, immediately at the onset of an attack.

3. Ergotamine is no longer favoured in emergency, and metoclopramide injection is preferred.

4. Metoclopramide caution: extrapyramidal effects especially in young people, particularly females.

5. Clonidine, propranolol, and pizotifen are alternative prophylactic drugs.

6. Clonidine can cause dry mouth and sleeplessness and may aggravate depression.

7. Propranolol can cause bronchospasm, peripheral vasoconstriction, and heart failure.
8. Pizotifen can cause weight gain and anticholinergic side-effects.

Cost

Soluble aspirin	300 mg	100 tabs =	35p
Soluble paracetamol	500 mg	100 tabs =	£4.08
	250 mg/5 ml suspension	500 ml =	£4.20
Metoclopramide	10 mg	100 tabs =	£5.13
	5 mg/5 ml syrup	500 ml =	£5.25
	10 mg/2 ml injection	10 amps =	£1.67
Clonidine	25 micrograms	100 tabs =	£5.11
Propranolol	40 mg	100 tabs =	25p
Pizotifen	500 micrograms	100 tabs =	£7.82
	1.5 mg	100 tabs =	£27.93

Mouth infections

Mouth ulcers

Treatment

Hydrocortisone lozenges — Adult and child dose: 2.5 mg dissolved slowly in the mouth in close contact with the ulcer, four times daily.

Oral candidiasis

Treatment

Nystatin mixture — Child dose: Instil 1 ml (100 000 units/ml) in the mouth after food, four times daily.

| Amphotericin lozenges | Adult dose: | Dissolve 10 mg lozenge slowly in mouth four times daily. |

Important notes

1. Nystatin mixture should not be washed away with drinks.
2. Treatment should continue for 2 days after the infection is cleared.

Oral and perioral herpes

Treatment

| Idoxuridine 0.1% drops | Adults and older children: | Hold 2 ml in contact with lesions for 3 minutes four times daily. |
| | Younger children: | Paint lesions four times daily. |

Important notes

1. Oral and perioral herpes do not usually require specific treatment.

2. There is concern that the use of acyclovir for the treatment of such minor conditions may lead to the development of drug-resistant viruses.

3. Idoxuridine 0.1 per cent drops are the eye-drops and not the skin paint.

Dental abscess

Treatment

| Penicillin V or | Adult dose: Child dose: | 250 mg four times daily. 1–5 years: 125 mg four times daily; 6–12 years: 250 mg four times daily. |
| Ampicillin | Adult dose: Child dose: | 250 mg four times daily. 1–12 years: 125 mg four times daily. |

Important notes

1. Most dental infections seem to respond to simple penicillin; however, some doctors prefer a broad-spectrum penicillin.

2. Erythromycin or co-trimoxazole may be used for patients allergic to penicillin.

3. Metronidazole may be given if anaerobic infection is suspected or if the condition fails to respond to penicillin.

Cost

Hydrocortisone lozenges	2.5 mg	100 tabs	= £7.00
Nystatin mixture	100 000 units/ml	30 ml	= £2.27
Amphotericin lozenges	10 mg	100 tabs	= £6.00
Idoxuridine 0.1% drops		15 ml	= £3.35
Penicillin V	125 mg	100 tabs	= 65p
	250 mg	100 tabs	= £1.27
	125 mg/5 ml elixir	500 ml	= £2.40
Ampicillin	250 mg	100 caps	= £2.99
	125 mg/5 ml mixture	500 ml	= £2.45

Nausea and/or Vomiting and/or Vertigo

Treatment

Prochlorperazine	Adult dose:	12.5–25 mg immediately in acute vomiting/vertigo, then 5–10 mg orally 2–4 hours later. Maintenance dose

		5 mg three times daily.
Child dose:		1-5 years: 2.5 mg twice daily;
		6-12 years 5 mg twice to three times daily.

Important notes

1. Check cause of nausea, vomiting, or vertigo.

2. Prochlorperazine may cause dry mouth and sedation, particularly with alcohol, mainly in high dosage. It can also cause extrapyramidal effects especially in young people, particularly females.

3. It can cause hypotension in elderly patients.

4. Initial dosage to adults can be either 12.5 mg by intramuscular injection or 25 mg rectally as a suppository. In severe vomiting a child may be given a 5 mg suppository.

Cost

Prochlorperazine	5 mg	100 tabs	= £3.92
	10 mg	100 tabs	= £3.73
	5 mg/5 ml syrup	500 ml	= £5.16
	5 mg suppos	10 suppos	= £3.40
	25 mg suppos	10 suppos	= £4.47
	12.5 mg/ml injection	10 × 1 ml	= £2.66

Neurological disorders

Epilepsy

Treatment

Phenytoin	Adult dose:	150-300 mg daily can be increased slowly to 600 mg.

| Carbamazepine | Adult dose: | 100–200 mg once or twice daily, can be increased to 0.8– 1.2 g daily. |

Important notes

1. General practitioners do not normally initiate the treatment of epilepsy except in known cases of cerebrovascular or neoplastic disease in adults.

2. Both drugs can cause dizziness, drowsiness, and gastrointestinal disturbance.

3. Phenytoin can cause headache, confusion, and insomnia. It can also cause a variety of skin problems, gingival hypertrophy, and anaemia due to folate deficiency.

4. Carbamazepine can cause a generalized erythmatous skin rash in 3 per cent of patients, and leucopenia can rarely occur.

5. Correct dosages can only be achieved by monitoring plasma concentration.

Neuralgia

Treatment

| Analgesics | *See under* Pain. |
| Carbamazepine | As above |

Important note

1. Tricyclic antidepressants may be valuable in treating post-herpetic neuralgia.

Raised intracranial pressure

Treatment

| Dexamethasone | Adult dose: | 500 micrograms to 16 mg daily, in divided doses. |

Important notes

1. Treatment should not be started before specific diagnosis is confirmed.

2. Dexamethasone is a corticosteroid. For side-effects, *see under* Asthma.

Spasticity

Treatment

Diazepam	Adult dose:	2 mg three times daily.
Baclofen	Adult dose:	5–30 mg three times daily.

Important notes

1. Diazepam is a benzodiazepine. For side-effects, *see under* Anxiety.

2. Baclofen may cause nausea, vomiting, fatigue, and hypotension. It should be used with caution in patients with psychiatric illness and cerebrovascular disease.

Parkinsonism

Treatment

Benzhexol	Adult dose:	1 mg daily, gradually increased to 5–15 mg daily, in three or four divided doses.
Orphenadrine	Adult dose:	150 mg gradually increased to maximum 400 mg, in three or four divided doses.
Sinemet	Adult dose:	100 mg levodopa three or four times daily, increased to 750 mg to 1.5 g, in divided doses.

Madopar	Adult dose:	50–100 mg twice daily, increased to 400–800 mg, in divided doses.

Important notes

1. Identify causative drugs (e.g. phenothiazines, methyldopa) and eliminate if possible.

2. Anticholinergics (benzhexol, orphenadrine) should be used with care in patients with prostatic disease, glaucoma, hepatic or renal impairment. Dry mouth may be a problem and cardiovascular disease may be a contraindication.

3. Benzhexol and orphenadrine are usually used to counteract phenothiazine side-effects.

4. Sinemet is a combination of levodopa and carbidopa, and Madopar is a combination of levodopa and benserazide. Doses are expressed as levodopa.

5. Levodopa appears to have a limited span of therapeutic effect and its use should be reserved and carefully evaluated. Its side-effects include anorexia, nausea, insomnia, cardiac arrhythmias, hypotension, discoloration of body fluids, and abnormal movements, as well as psychiatric symptoms.

6. Levodopa preparations should be used with caution in patients suffering from peptic ulcer, cardiovascular disease, diabetes, open-angle glaucoma, skin melanoma, and psychiatric illness.

Cost

Phenytoin	25 mg	100 caps = £1.70
Carbamazepine	100 mg	100 tabs = £2.90
	200 mg	100 tabs = £5.38
	400 mg	100 tabs = £10.58
Dexamethasone	500 micrograms	100 tabs = £3.19
	2 mg	100 tabs = £10.95
Diazepam	2 mg	100 tabs = 12p
Baclofen	10 mg	100 tabs = £12.99
Benhexol	2 mg	100 tabs = £1.86
	5 mg	100 tabs = £3.62

Orphenadrine	50 mg	100 tabs = £1.48
Sinemet	'110' 100 mg levodopa	100 tabs = £8.55
	'Plus' 100 mg levodopa	100 tabs = £11.64
	'275' 250 mg levodopa	100 tabs = £17.87
Madopar	'62.5' 50 mg levodopa	100 tabs = £5.94
	'125' 100 mg levodopa	100 tabs = £10.72
	'250' 200 mg levodopa	100 tabs = £18.34

Otitis externa

Treatment

Locorten-vioform drops   Adult and child dose: Instil 2-3 drops twice daily.

Important notes

1. Caution: local effects due to strong steroid preparations. Fungal overgrowth and local sensitivity reactions may occur with prolonged use of anti-infective agents.

2. Locorten-vioform is a mixture of clioquinol 1 per cent and flumethasone piranate 0.02 per cent.

Ear wax

Treatment

Olive-oil drops   Adult and child dose: Instil 2 drops four times daily.

Important note

1. In the event of suspected otitis media ear-drops are contraindicated and a suitable oral antibiotic should be given (see Upper respiratory tract infection).

Cost

Locorten-vioform	7.5 ml = £1.05
Olive oil	10 ml = 5p

Pain

Treatment

Soluble aspirin	Adult dose:	300–600 mg four/six-hourly as necessary.
	Child dose:	Contraindicated for children under 12 years of age.
Paracetamol	Adult dose:	500 mg to 1 g four/six-hourly as necessary.
	Child dose:	Under 3 months: not recommended. 3 months to 1 year: 60–120 mg; 1–6 years: 120–240 mg; 6–12 years: 250–500 mg. All six-hourly as necessary.
Aspirin and codeine	Adult dose:	1–2 four/six-hourly as necessary.
	Child dose:	Not suitable for children.
Codeine and paracetamol	Adult dose:	1–2 four/six-hourly as necessary.
Codeine phosphate	Adult dose:	15–60 mg four/six-hourly as necessary.
Dihydrocodeine and paracetamol	Adult dose:	1–2 four/six-hourly as necessary.

Dihydrocodeine	Adult dose:	30–60 mg four/six-hourly as necessary.
Pethidine	Adult dose:	50–150 mg four-hourly as necessary.
Morphine sulphate s.r.*	Adult dose:	10–20 mg twice daily as necessary.
Diamorphine*	Adult dose:	10 mg six-hourly as necessary.
Morphine* or Diamorphine in chloroform water or Prochlorperazine or Chlorpromazine elixir	Adult dose:	5 ml six-hourly as necessary.
Morphine* (injection)	Adult dose:	10 mg four-hourly, increasing as necessary.
Diamorphine* (injection)	Adult dose:	5 mg four-hourly, increasing as necessary.

Important notes

1. Arranged in escalating order of analgesic potency and acceptability.

2. In cancer, metastatic bone pain may show good response to non-steroidal anti-inflammatory drugs with antiprostaglandin activity, e.g. indomethacin. As nausea is also a frequent side-effect anti-emetics such as prochlorperazine are often useful and some morphine injections are combined with cyclizine for this benefit (i.e. cyclimorph).

3. Dextropropoxyphene, a previously popular analgesic, is not included as it is especially dangerous in overdose, particularly with alcohol, and may even be harmful in any debilitated patient in normal doses.

4. Respiratory depression with narcotic analgesics is a common

side-effect. Dependency is only a signficant possibility in long-term usage in non-terminal conditions.

5. Constipation can be caused by all strong analgesics.

*6. Dose and frequency of administration of analgesics for terminal pain should be increased to prevent recurrence of pain.

7. Aspirin must not be given to children under 12 years old.

8. Pethidine is mainly for use in renal colic and childbirth.

9. Morphine or diamorphine elixir can be made up with 5 mg upwards of morphine diluted in 5 ml chloroform water or prochlorperazine or chlorpromazine syrup. The strength of all components can be increased as is appropriate for pain or nausea.

Cramp pain

Treatment

Quinine sulphate   Adult dose: 300 mg at night.

Important note

The dose should not be exceeded and no other pain is helped by quinine sulphate. Side-effects are rare at this dose, but can include abdominal pain, nausea, and headaches.

Cost

Soluble aspirin	300 mg	100 tabs =	35p
Paracetamol	500 mg	100 tabs =	35p
	120 mg/5 ml suspension	500 ml =	£3.35
Aspirin and codeine		100 tabs =	94p
Codeine and paracetamol		100 tabs =	£2.46
Codeine phosphate	30 mg	100 tabs =	£1.73
Dihydrocodeine and paracetamol		100 tabs =	£1.77
Dihydrocodeine	30 mg	100 tabs =	£3.78
	10 mg/5 ml elixir	500 ml =	£4.27

Pethidine hydrochloride	50 mg	100 tabs = £1.46
Morphine sulphate s.r.	10 mg	100 tabs = £12.83
	30 mg	100 tabs = £30.82
	60 mg	100 tabs = £60.01
	100 mg	100 tabs = £95.83
Diamorphine hydrochloride	10 mg	100 tabs = £4.39
Morphine sulphate	10 mg injection	10 amps = £2.64
	15 mg injection	10 amps = £2.74
	30 mg injection	10 amps = £2.96
Diamorphine hydrochloride	5 mg injection	10 amps = £7.16
	10 mg injection	10 amps = £7.52
	30 mg injection	10 amps = £8.18
	100 mg injection	10 amps = £24.12
Quinine sulphate	300 mg	100 tabs = £2.64

Premenstrual syndrome

Treatment

Bendrofluazide	Adult dose:	5 mg daily on days 16–28 of menstrual cycle.
Pyridoxine	Adult dose:	50 mg twice daily on days 16–28 of menstrual cycle.
Norethisterone	Adult dose:	5 mg twice daily on days 19–26 of menstrual cycle.
Dydrogesterone	Adult dose:	10 mg twice daily on days 12–26 of menstrual cycle.

Important notes

1. Salt restriction and/or a diuretic may be useful for bloating.
2. Pyridoxine is useful for depression and irritation.
3. Be aware that premenstrual syndrome can be a symptom of other psychiatric or psychosexual problems.
4. Norethisterone and dydrogesterone should be used with caution in diabetes, hypertension, and hepatic or renal disease, and may cause acne, urticaria, oedema, gastrointestinal upsets, changes in libido, breast discomfort, and irregular menstruation.

Dysmenorrhoea

Treatment

Mefenamic acid	Adult dose:	250–500 mg three times daily.
Dydrogesterone	Adult dose:	10 mg twice daily on days 5–12 of menstrual cycle.

Important notes

1. Mefenamic acid may be better than simple analgesics.
2. Mefenamic acid can cause gastric irritation, hypersensitivity reactions (including asthma), headache, drowsiness, renal impairment, rashes, and blood dyscrasias.

Cost

Bendrofluazide	5 mg	100 tabs =	21p
Pyridoxine	50 mg	100 tabs =	£2.60
Norethisterone	5 mg	100 tabs =	£10.78
Dydrogesterone	10 mg	100 tabs =	£16.75
Mefenamic acid	250 mg	100 tabs =	£5.65
	500 mg	100 tabs =	£10.32

Pruritus vulvae and vaginal discharge

Treatment

Nystatin pessaries	Adult:	1 pessary (100 000 units) to be inserted at night for 14 nights.
Clotrimazole pessaries	Adult:	100 mg at night for 6 nights, or 200 mg at night for 3 nights, or 500 mg at night, once only.
Metronidazole	Adult:	400 mg twice daily for 5–7 days.
Nystatin cream	Adult:	100 000 units/g, apply twice daily.
Clotrimazole cream 1%	Adult:	Apply twice daily.

Important notes

1. Ideally, high vaginal and cervical swabs should be taken to exclude/discover trichomonal or other venereal infection. If no response to treatment, swabs are essential.

2. Consider treating partner or suggest he sees his own doctor.

3. Diabetes, pregnancy, steroids, antibiotics, and the pill are pre-disposing causes of candidiasis, and recurrence is more likely in these conditions.

4. Nystatin and clotrimazole creams may be used in combination with pessaries for associated vulvitis (or partner's balanitis).

5. Nystatin and clotrimazole creams may produce local irritation.

6. Metronidazole produces similar impairment with alcohol as disulfiram. Alcohol must not be taken. It should not be used in pregnancy or breast-feeding. Side-effects include gastrointestinal disturbances, headache, vertigo, ataxia, confusion, seizures, peripheral neuropathy, skin rashes, and neutropenia.

Cost

Nystatin pessaries with applicator		15 pessaries = £1.09
Clotrimazole pessaries with applicator	100 mg	6 pessaries = £2.64
	200 mg	3 pessaries = £2.58
	500 mg	1 pessary = £2.58
Metronidazole	200 mg	100 tabs = £6.68
Nystatin cream		60 g = £3.26
Clotrimazole cream		20 g = £1.82

Skin conditions

Acute eczema/Dermatitis

Treatment

Betamethasone
0.1% cream or
ointment
Adult and child dose: Apply twice daily.

Dry eczema/Ichthyosis

Treatment

Aqueous cream	Adult and child:	Apply twice daily.
Hydrocortisone 1% ointment	Adult and child:	Apply twice daily.
Emulsifying ointment	Adult and child:	Use as soap substitute in the bath.
Dimethicone cream	Adult and child:	Use as a barrier cream.

Nappy rash

Treatment

Zinc cream	All ages:	Apply with each nappy change.
Nystaform HC cream	All ages:	Apply twice daily.

Psoriasis

Treatment

Alphosyl cream	Adult and child:	Apply up to four times daily.
Dithrocream (0.1%, 0.25%)	Adult and child:	Apply for 30 minutes daily in increasing strengths.
Betamethasone 0.025% cream or ointment	Adult and child:	Apply daily.
Polytar liquid	Adult and child:	Shampoo twice weekly.

Important notes

1. Creams are either water-miscible and easily washed off, or oily. They tend to moisten the skin, although modern ointment bases have occlusive properties on the skin surface and may encourage hydration.

2. Potent steroid preparations damage subcutaneous collagen and should never be used on the face.

3. Nystaform HC cream is a combination of hydrocortisone 0.05 per cent, nystatin 100 000 u/g, and chlorhexidine 1 per cent.

4. Alphosyl cream is a combination of coal-tar extract 5 per cent and allantoin 2 per cent.

5. Dithrocream may produce local burning sensation and stain skin, hair, and clothing. Treatment should be started with the weakest preparation, and the strength increased as tolerated.

Cost

Alphosyl cream		75 g	= £1.56
Aqueous cream		100 g	= 22p
Betamethasone 0.1% cream or ointment		100 g	= £3.51
Betamethasone 0.025% cream or ointment		100 g	= £2.90
Dimethicone cream		100 g	= 52p
Dithrocream	0.1%	100 g	= £6.26
	0.25%	100 g	= £6.74
Emulsifying ointment		100 g	= 23p
Hydrocortisone 1% ointment		100 g	= £1.92
Nystaform HC cream		30 g	= £2.73
Polytar liquid		350 ml	= £2.37
Zinc cream		100 g	= 32p

Skin infections

Impetigo

Treatment

Chlortetracycline 3% cream	Adult and child:	Apply twice daily.
Flucloxacillin	Adult dose:	250 mg four times daily.
	Child dose:	Up to 2 years: 62.5 mg four times daily; 2–10 years: 125 mg. Both four times daily.

Important note

Systemic antibiotics are usually unnecessary for impetigo.

Cellulitis

Treatment

Penicillin V	Adult dose:	250–500 mg four times daily.
	Child dose:	Up to 1 year: 62.5 mg; 1–5 years: 125 mg; 6–12 years: 250 mg. All four times daily.
Flucloxacillin	Adult dose:	250–500 mg four times daily.
	Child dose:	Up to 1 year: 62.5 mg; 1–5 years: 125 mg; 6–12 years: 250 mg. All four times daily.

Erysipelas

Treatment

Penicillin V	Adult dose:	250–500 mg four times daily.
	Child dose:	Up to 1 year: 62.5 mg; 1–5 years: 125 mg; 6–12 years: 250 mg. All four times daily.

Acne vulgaris

Treatment

Oxytetracycline	Adult dose:	250 mg four times daily for 1–4 weeks, then twice daily as long as condition recurs.

	Child dose:	Inappropriate under 12 years of age.
Co-trimoxazole	Adult dose:	480 mg twice daily for 1–4 weeks, then once daily as long as condition recurs.
	Child dose:	Inappropriate under 12 years of age.
Erythromycin	Adult dose:	250 mg four times daily for 1–4 weeks, then twice daily as long as condition recurs.
Benzoyl peroxide 5% lotion		Apply daily after cleansing.

Important notes

1. For side-effects of oxytetracycline, co-trimoxazole, and erythromycin, *see under* Bronchitis. Be particularly aware of possibility of pregnancy in young women.

2. Long-term use of co-trimoxazole may lead to folic-acid deficiency.

3. Organisms resistant to all antibiotics particularly erythromycin may occur with long-term use.

4. Benzoyl peroxide may be used alone or in addition to one of the antibiotics suggested.

Scabies

Treatment

| Benzyl benzoate 25% application | Adult dose: | Apply two nights running, over whole body except neck and head. |
| Lindane 1% lotion | Child dose: | Apply once, over whole body except neck and head. Repeat in five days. |

Important notes

1. The irritation of scabies is a hypersensitivity-response to the insect's waste products. It can be present without apparent itching. Look for burrows.

2. Benzyl benzoate is itself irritating to skin and children are better treated with lindane.

Tinea

Treatment

Whitfield's ointment	Adult and child:	Apply twice daily.
Clotrimazole 1% cream	Adult and child:	Apply twice daily.

Herpes simplex

Treatment

Betadine paint (povidone-iodine 10%)	Adult and child:	Apply twice daily.

Herpes zoster

Treatment

Idoxuridine 5% application	Adult and child:	Apply four times daily for 5 days.

Warts

Treatment

Salicyclic acid collodion	Adult and child:	Apply daily.

Cost

Benzoyl peroxide	5% lotion	150 ml	=	£5.25
Benzyl benzoate	25% application	500 ml	=	£1.51

Betadine paint		8 ml	=	63p
Chlortetracycline	3% cream	30 g	=	£1.82
Clotrimazole	1% cream	20 g	=	£1.82
Co-trimoxazole	480 mg	100 tabs	=	£4.00
	240 mg/5 ml suspension	500 ml	=	£8.00
Erythromycin	250 mg	100 tabs	=	£4.50
	250 mg/5 ml suspension	500 ml	=	£11.15
	500 mg/5 ml suspension	500 ml	=	£21.30
Flucloxacillin	250 mg	100 caps	=	£20.10
	500 mg	100 caps	=	£40.20
	125 mg/5 ml syrup	500 ml	=	£16.60
Idoxuridine	5% application	5 ml	=	£4.90
Lindane	1% lotion	500 ml	=	£2.08
Oxytetracycline	250 mg	100 tabs	=	£1.08
Penicillin V	125 mg	100 tabs	=	65p
	250 mg	100 tabs	=	£1.27
Salicyclic acid collodion		5 ml	=	5p
Whitfield's ointment		100 g	=	59p

Upper respiratory tract infections

The common cold

Treatment

Needs no specific treatment.

Catarrh

Treatment

Steam inhalations		Three-hourly as required.
Pseudoephedrine	Adult dose:	60 mg three times daily.
	Child dose:	Under 3 months: not recommended; 3 months to 1 year: 2.5 ml; 1–6 years: 5 ml; 6–12 years: 7.5 ml. All three times daily.

Important notes

1. At least two weeks blocked nose without pain or purulent discharge = catarrh.

2. Beware allergies, sinusitis, polyps.

3. Fresh air and lower setting on central heating may be most effective treatment.

4. Hot water (not boiling) for inhalation. Beware spilling, particularly for elderly people and children.

5. Pseudoephedrine should be avoided in patients with hypertension, hyperthyroidism, coronary heart disease, and diabetes. It is totally contraindicated for patients on MAOI inhibitors.

Cough

Treatment

Linctus codeine	Adult dose:	5–10 ml up to four times daily.
Linctus codeine paediatric	Child dose:	Up to 1 year: 5 ml; 1–5 years: 10 ml. Up to four times daily.
Linctus simplex	Adult dose:	5–10 ml up to four times daily.

| Linctus simplex paediatric | Child dose: | 5–10 ml up to four times daily. |

Important note

Simple linctus is palliative for sore throats but codeine linctus is a cough suppressant and should not be used if a cough is productive.

Sinusitis

Treatment

Ampicillin	Adult dose:	250–500 mg four times daily.
	Child dose:	125–250 mg four times daily.
Erythromycin	Adult dose:	250–500 mg four times daily.
	Child dose:	Under 2 years: 125 mg; 2–8 years: 250 mg; Over 8 years: 250 mg. All four times daily.

Important notes

1. For patients allergic to penicillins, erythromycin is a suitable alternative.

2. For side-effects of ampicillin and erythromycin, *see under* Bronchitis.

Throat infections

Treatment

| Paracetamol | Adult dose: | 500 mg four/six-hourly as necessary. |
| | Child dose: | Under 1 year: 60–120 mg; 1–5 years: 120–250 mg; 6–12 years: 250–500 mg. All four times daily. |

Penicillin V	Adult dose:	250–500 mg four times daily.
	Child dose:	Under 1 year: 62.5 mg; 1–5 years: 125 mg; 6–12 years: 250 mg. All four times daily.
Erythromycin	Adult dose:	250–500 mg four times daily.
	Child dose:	Under 2 years: 125 mg; 2–8 years: 250 mg; Over 8 years: 250 mg. All four times daily.

Important notes

1. 70 per cent or more of throat infections are viral and require only symptomatic treatment.

2. Paracetamol is to treat discomfort and pyrexia only, and may be used in viral or bacterial conditions.

3. Penicillin V is the treatment of choice for bacterial conditions, and erythromycin the first alternative if the patient is allergic to penicillin.

4. Side-effects of penicillin and erythromycin are listed in the section on bronchitis.

Otitis media

Treatment

Ampicillin	Adult dose:	500 mg four times daily.
	Child dose:	250 mg four times daily.
Amoxycillin	Adult dose:	250–500 mg three times daily.
	Child dose:	Under 10 years: 125 mg three times daily.
Co-trimoxazole	Adult dose:	960 mg twice daily.
	Child dose:	6 weeks to 6 months: 120 mg twice daily; 6 months to 5 years: 240 mg twice daily;

		6-12 years: 480 mg twice daily.
Erythromycin	Adult dose:	250-500 mg four times daily.
	Child dose:	Under 2 years: 125 mg; 2-8 years: 250 mg; Over 8 years: 250 mg. All four times daily.

Important notes

1. Amoxycillin and ampicillin have identical spectrum of antibacterial activity. Amoxycillin is only indicated in treatment of acute otitis media in children under 3 years of age.

2. Side-effects of amoxycillin and ampicillin are similar although diarrhoea is less common with amoxycillin. For side-effects of other antibiotics, *see under* Bronchitis.

Cost

Steam inhalations		Free		
Pseudoephedrine	60 mg	100 tabs	=	£4.42
	30 mg/5 ml syrup	500 ml	=	£3.55
Codeine linctus		500 ml	=	£1.31
Codeine linctus paediatric		500 ml	=	85p
Simple linctus		500 ml	=	72p
Simple linctus paediatric		500 ml	=	76p
Ampicillin	250 mg	100 caps	=	£2.99
	500 mg	100 caps	=	£5.92
	125 mg/5 ml suspension	500 ml	=	£2.45
	250 mg/5 ml suspension	500 ml	=	£4.60
Paracetamol	500 g	100 tabs	=	35p
	120 mg/5 ml suspension	500 ml	=	£3.35

Penicillin V	125 mg	100 tabs	=	65p
	250 mg	100 tabs	=	£1.27
	62.5 mg/5 ml syrup	500 ml	=	£2.20
	125 mg/5 ml	500 ml	=	£2.40
	250 mg/5 ml	500 ml	=	£4.45
Amoxycillin	250 mg	100 caps	=	£16.61
	500 mg	100 caps	=	£33.21
	125 mg/5 ml syrup	100 ml	=	£7.84
	250 mg/5 ml	100 ml	=	£14.68
Co-trimoxazole	480 mg	100 tabs	=	£4.00
	240 mg/5 ml suspension	500 ml	=	£8.00
Erythromycin	250 mg	100 tabs	=	£4.50
	500 mg	100 tabs	=	£20.67
	125 mg/5 ml suspension	500 ml	=	£7.40
	250 mg/5 ml suspension	500 ml	=	£11.15
	500 mg/5 ml suspension	500 ml	=	£21.30

Urinary tract conditions

Acute infection

Treatment

Trimethoprim	Adult dose:	200 mg twice daily.
	Child dose:	2–5 months: 25 mg twice daily;
		6 months to 5 years: 50 mg twice daily;
		6–12 years: 100 mg twice daily.

Co-trimoxazole	Adult dose:	960 mg twice daily.
	Child dose:	6 weeks to 6 months: 120 mg twice daily; 6 months to 5 years: 240 mg twice daily; 6–12 years: 480 mg twice daily.
Ampicillin	Adult dose:	500 mg four times daily.
	Child dose:	250 mg four times daily.
Nitrofurantoin	Adult dose:	100 mg four times daily.
	Child dose:	3 months to 2 years: 12.5 mg four times daily; 2–6 years: 25 mg four times daily; 6–11 years: 50 mg four times daily; 11–14 years: 75 mg four times daily.

Important notes

1. Ideally, send MSU before and after treatment.

2. Trimethoprim may cause gastrointestinal disturbances, nausea, vomiting, pruritus, rashes, depression of haemopoiesis.

3. Co-trimoxazole may cause nausea, vomiting, rashes, and blood dyscrasias (*see under* Bronchitis).

4. Ampicillin side-effects include urticaria, fever, joint pains, angio-neurotic oedema, anaphylactic shock in hypersensitive patients, diarrhoea, erythematous rashes in glandular fever.

5. Nitrofurantoin may cause nausea, vomiting, rashes, peripheral neuropathy, pulmonary infiltration, allergic liver damage.

6. The treatments suggested are alternatives, and should cure most infections, and cover most allergic problems in patients.

Enuresis
Treatment

Imipramine	Child dose:	Over 6 years: 25–50 mg at night.

Detrusor instability
Treatment

Imipramine	Adult dose:	25 mg three times daily.

Urinary frequency and incontinence
Treatment

Emepronium bromide	Adult dose:	200 mg three times daily or 400 mg at night.

Important notes

1. Imipramine may cause dry mouth and other anticholinergic side-effects. Also tachycardia, sweating, and sometimes sleep disturbances in children. Other side-effects at this dosage are rare.

2. Emepronium bromide may cause anticholinergic side-effects. Beware particularly of prostatic obstruction and glaucoma.

Cost

Trimethoprim	100 mg	100 tabs	= £2.30
	200 mg	100 tabs	= £3.75
	50 mg/5 ml suspension	100 ml	= £1.36
Co-trimoxazole	480 mg	100 tabs	= £4.00
	240 mg/5 ml suspension	500 ml	= £8.00
Ampicillin	250 mg	100 caps	= £2.99
	500 mg	100 caps	= £5.92
	125 mg/5 ml suspension	500 ml	= £2.45
	250 mg/5 ml syrup	500 ml	= £4.60

Nitrofurantoin	50 mg	100 tabs	= £3.75
	100 mg	100 tabs	= £7.10
	25 mg/5 ml suspension	500 ml	= £7.50
Imipramine	10 mg	100 tabs	= 54p
	25 mg	100 tabs	= 50p
	25 mg/5 ml syrup	500 ml	= £9.00
Emepronium bromide	100 mg	100 tabs	= £6.70

Worms

Treatment

Pripsen	Adult dose:	One sachet.
(piperazine 4 g sennosides 15.3 mg)	Child dose:	3 months to 1 year: 5 ml granules; 1–6 years: 10 ml granules; Over 6 years: one sachet. Repeat all after 14 days.
Mebendazole	Adult dose:	100 mg.
	Child dose:	Over 2 years: 100 mg. Repeat after 14 days.

Important notes

1. Treat whole family.

2. Beware nail-biters and thumb suckers.

3. Pripsen may cause nausea, vomiting, diarrhoea, urticaria, rarely dizziness, paraesthesia, muscular incoordination.

4. Mebendazole occasionally causes abdominal pain, diarrhoea.

5. Both preparations have been found to be teratogenic in animals and should not be used if pregnancy is a possibility.

Cost

Pripsen sachets	piperazine 4 g sennosides 15.3 mg	2 sachets = 52p	
Mebendazole	100 mg	2 tabs	= 69p
	100 mg/5 ml suspension	10 ml	= 78p

Appendix

Drug treatments normally initiated by hospital consultants

Carcinoma of breast

| Tamoxifen | 10–40 mg twice daily. |

Epilepsy

1. Phenobarbitone	15–300 mg at night.
2. Primidone	125–500 mg three times daily.
3. Sodium valproate	100–500 mg three times daily.

Glaucoma

| 1. Pilocarpine eye-drops | Apply 3–6 times daily. |
| 2. Timolol eye-drops | Apply twice daily. |

Hypertension

| Captopril | 25–50 mg three times daily. |

Manic depression

Lithium carbonate   250 mg to 2 g daily.

Peptic ulcer

Ranitidine   150 mg twice daily.

Prophylaxis in pregnancy

Iron and Folic acid   One daily.

Thrombo-embolism/Platelet disorders

1. Warfarin   3–9 mg daily.
2. Dipyridamole   100–200 mg three times
                                         daily.

Important notes

1. We have not attempted to include all the various insulins, dressings, stoma equipment, etc.

2. Dosage can be continued as repeat prescriptions under hospital direction.

Index